OFFICIAL FORTNITE

THE CHRONICLE 2022

CONTENTS

TO THE BATTLE BUS!

Fortnite has taken gamers on an epic journey ever since 2017. From Quests and Challenges to Battle Pass rewards, map changes, awesome new Outfits and even competitive tournaments, the game is constantly evolving. Question is, can you keep pace?

Luckily, this book is here to help and guide you. The pages are packed with all the big Battle Royale events, characters, changes, and stories. Looking back over the past 12 months, you'll relive the major surprises and memorable moments the Fortnite community has experienced.

It's time to head to the Battle Bus, because this is going to be quite a ride.

LET THE BATTLE ROYALE BEGIN!

CHOOSE YOUR LANDING SPOT AND PREPARE TO TEST YOUR KNOWLEDGE

Every day, millions enjoy exploring the Island as Fortnite continues to innovate and lead the way. It gives gamers the chance to take on a thrilling quest and be the best, but how exactly does it keep doing this Season after Season? Turn the page to explore more...

FORTNITE FOREVER

CHANGING TIMES

While the essence of Fortnite stays the same, with 100 players dropping onto the Island and the last player or team standing taking the Victory Royale, the game still advances and unfolds in special ways. New Seasons deliver new dynamics, items, Outfits, and, in recent Seasons, game changers like trucks and sports cars, wild animals, and advantageous fishing. Fortnite never stands still, and you shouldn't either.

KEEPING IN TOUCH

Hook up with your friends for a fun and exciting Fortnite experience. Regardless of whether you play on PC, mobile, or console, the game's cross-platform support keeps you all in touch and lets you tackle the opposition together. Party Royale is also a great space for you to hang out, watch movies, and enjoy special events in a combat-free zone. Also, the ability to video chat in Fortnite via the Houseparty app arrived in Chapter 2 Season 4 as another neat way for gamers to connect with their friends.

COMMUNITY DRIVEN

The Fortnite community has a huge voice and Epic is always interested in hearing the feedback of its players. The game is updated regularly, sees incredible content developed in Fortnite Creative, offers recurring Ventures Seasons in Save the World, and with frequent competitive events—such as the Fortnite Champion Series (FNCS) and Friday Nite Dragging Rights—there's always something new to check out. It's a lively and inclusive crowd made up of players from every corner of the planet.

REACH THE LIMITS

From The Spy Within to Air Royale, Bodyguard, Rally Royale, and Tilted Taxis, new Limited Time Modes have appeared and amazed throughout Chapter 2. Known as LTMs, these special modes join the game for just a few weeks or days at a time. As fans encounter the new rules they bring, the action heats up as tactics and techniques are mastered. When an LTM appears in the mode select menu, you know things are going to get hectic!

YOU DO YOU!

Fortnite is all about what you want to do, what you achieve, and the path you want to explore. Even if you don't achieve the same feats as those of a high-profile streamer or FNCS winner, every player can enjoy some serious fun and soak up what it means to be a part of the world's coolest game. Battle Royale is open to all, so grab your weapon and decide what your story will be today!

A NEW CHAPTER

CHAPTER 2's EVOLVING ISLAND

Over the last year, Chapter 2 has seen stacks of updates, additions, and changes. It has brought us the shifting crystalline sands in Season 5 and the autumnal orange biome in Season 6, Characters offering Quests and items, an Island currency made of gold (Bars), special Exotic items, and even Crafting using Animal Bones and Mechanical Parts. Throw in a stash of superheroes, fearsome Loot Sharks, Marauders, and a helping of spies, and Chapter 2 has been full of shocks and surprises along the way.

Among other things, the happenings of Chapter 2 before the present time include the vast flood in Chapter 2 Season 3 and Spawn Island being taken over by a floating command ship in the following Season. Chapter 2 Season 6 saw the arrival of The Spire in the center of the map, with the primal biome stretching out from it.

The Battle Pass has taken on a fresh vibe throughout Chapter 2 as well. We've seen A.L.T.E.R. and E.G.O. Outfit Styles unlocked by completing Challenges, cool rewards like built-in Emotes and built-in Gliders, the Awakening Challenges of Season 4's superheroes, and the arrival of the Fortnite Crew subscription offer, which ensures that active subscribers always have access to the current Battle Pass. Now it's time to relive some of Chapter 2's events and headlines. How many of these do you remember?

PRIME TIME

WHEN THE ZERO POINT WAS SEALED IN STONE, THINGS GOT WILD

Chapter 2 Season 6 saw a new look, vibe, and story event sweep across the Island. The central Zero Point was suddenly encased in a giant stone tower—The Spire—after efforts from Agent Jones and The Foundation.

What could now be discovered through the Island included two more new Points of Interest (POIs): Colossal Crops to the east of The Spire and Boney Burbs to the west. As the Season's primal biome spread its reach in every direction, it brought with it a battle-primed wilderness. By venturing to the edges of its primal landscapes, you could find Guardian Spires protected by mysterious forces. Here, your primal instincts needed to be fully switched on.

Chapter 2 Season 6 was a wild time in every sense. Animals never seen before began to emerge on the scene, starting with wolves, chickens, boars, and frogs. All the while, though, there was an indication that the most fearsome predators had yet to hatch. Tense times, to say the least!

CHARACTER BUILDING

Island residents known as Characters populated the Island, starting in Chapter 2 Season 5. These included familiar faces such as Triggerfish, Bushranger, and Doggo. You could interact with a Character and accept their challenge to track down and eliminate a chosen enemy. This was called a Bounty. Complete your Bounty and rich rewards were on offer!

BEHIND BARS

Finishing the Bounty saw you pocket shiny Bars as your reward. Bars debuted as a new currency in Chapter 2 Season 5, existing for exchange on the Island.. Trade these golden delights with vendor Characters for items and upgrades!

KEEP COLLECTING

Bars were also available in other ways, such as discovering a hidden stash of the eye-catching treats as you explored your surroundings. Additionally, players could remain vigilant for Bars dropped by defeated opponents and earn Bars for completing Character-given Quests. Players could stash a maximum of 10,000 Bars in Chapter 2 Season 5.

HIRE LEVEL

Some Characters could also be hired after paying them 100 Bars for their service. In exchange, they would follow you around and become a combat ally and help protect you. Having Mancake or Mave, for example, by your side in the heat of a battle was a great boost.

DUEL DEAL

Feeling brave? Reckon you've brought your A-game? Instead of negotiating and befriending a Character, there was another route to take... challenge them to a duel. If successful, you'd walk away with a weapon, plus plenty of pride. Getting the better of someone mighty, like Brutus, was a sweet feeling.

ZERO POINTS THE WAY

Chapter 2 Season 5—a.k.a the Zero Point Season—saw Agent Jones recruiting Hunters to prevent anyone from escaping through the Zero Point. Left dangerously exposed after being destabilized, its energy created the crystalline, sinking desert zone around it, where it was possible to move quickly under the grains while hidden then spring a surprise on the enemy.

CRYSTAL CLEAR

Zero Point Crystals were foraged items from the desert around the Zero Point. They were used like a mini speed and teleport boost, but they didn't have any healing powers.

FLOODED FORTNITE

Who could forget what life on the Island was like when Chapter 2 Season 3 launched? After The Device event took place towards the end of Chapter 2 Season 2, the giant wall of water it created caused extensive flooding. In this new environment, players had to be prepared to dive in and embrace the aqua challenges all around them. With this new environment came new threats both above and below the surface. Luckily, sparkly new items and weapons appeared to help tackle these dangers.

LOOT SHARKS

With a Fishing Rod in-hand, savvy players mastered how to handle shark-infested waters—by catching a ride from one. These vicious sharks could also be defeated for loot.

ESSENTIAL EXTRAS

MARAUDERS

An AI enemy, Marauders descended from above in Chapter 2 Season 3 and stalked the Island ready for a fight.

BUILD-A-BRELLA

This customizable Brella Glider was one of the many reasons to go deep with your Battle Pass progress in Chapter 2 Season 3.

CHANGING SCENES

The water level receded and the landscape altered through the Season, revealing new locations and a new mode of transport.

JOIN THE CREW

Launched in Chapter 2 Season 5, Fortnite Crew is the ultimate monthly subscription offer. Included is the current Season's Battle Pass, 1,000 V-Bucks, and a monthly Fortnite Crew Pack with an always-new Outfit bundle, only for Crew Members.

EXTRA EXOTIC

Exotic-rarity weapons were introduced during Chapter 2. Taking a trip to see a Character and getting an Exotic weapon from them was a real highlight. Each Exotic has something special about it—it's well worth the effort to grab one.

GET COMPETITIVE

Whether it was the Fortnite Champion Series (FNCS), Cash Cups, Creator Cups, Friday Night Bragging Rights, or any other competition, Fortnite's competitive scene was as big as ever throughout Chapter 2.

NEXT GENERATION

Launched during Chapter 2 Season 4, the PlayStation 5, Xbox Series X, and Xbox Series S consoles allowed Fortnite players to harness next-gen power with enhanced dynamic visuals and physics. In the spirit of remembering the past while looking to the future, players on all Fortnite platforms had the chance to grab the Throwback Axe Pickaxe for free!

KNOW THE CODES

From build fights to box fights, Search & Destroy, Prop Hunt, and Capture the Flag, there are all sorts of maps to explore in Fortnite Creative. It's a great place to try different games and rules, so look out for popular Island Codes being highlighted regularly.

FORTNITE FACTS

- Fortnite Battle Royale's birthday is on September 26. It's a celebrated event each year—players have participated in special Challenges and taken up special items on the Island marking the big day!

- The Guided Missile was the first item to be unvaulted, back in Chapter 1 Season 5. It could also be ridden, in much the same way Rockets from the Rocket Launcher can.

- Bunker Chests arrived for the first time in Chapter 2 Season 6 and offered loot ranging from Rare to Legendary—including Rocket Launchers.

- Have you ever noticed that the powerful engine on top of the Battle Bus has the V-Bucks symbol on it? Take a look next time you get on board!

- At the end of Chapter 2 Season 4, a record 15.3 million players joined an in-game event all at the same time, and over 3.4 million watched on Twitch and YouTube. Staggering statistics!

- During Chapter 2 Season 2, it was revealed Fortnite had over 350 million registered players. In April 2020 alone, players spent more than 3.2 billion hours in-game.

- Bandolier was a Character on the Island in Chapter 2 Season 5, and in 2019, the first winner of the Community Choice vote. This vote saw the Outfit return to the Item Shop.

- In the "Arena" competitive mode, players earn Hype that correlates to their Arena Division Rank. Players need to reach Champion League (6,000 Hype) to be eligible for most competitive tournaments.

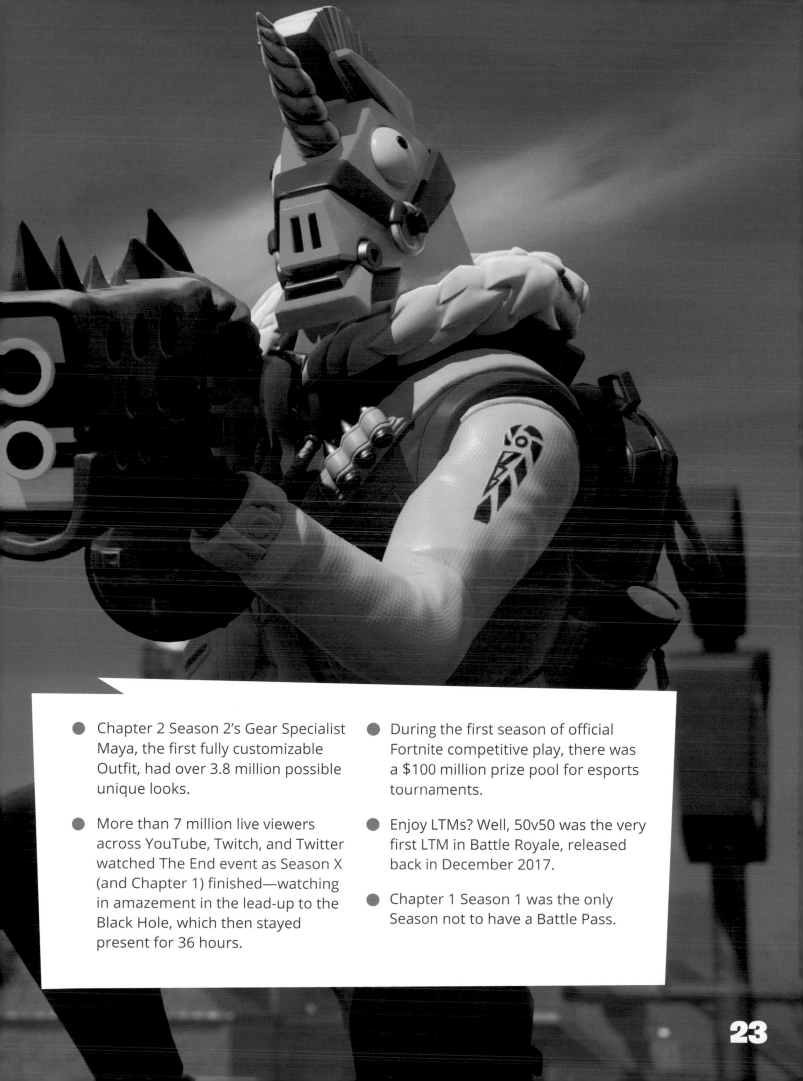

- Chapter 2 Season 2's Gear Specialist Maya, the first fully customizable Outfit, had over 3.8 million possible unique looks.

- More than 7 million live viewers across YouTube, Twitch, and Twitter watched The End event as Season X (and Chapter 1) finished—watching in amazement in the lead-up to the Black Hole, which then stayed present for 36 hours.

- During the first season of official Fortnite competitive play, there was a $100 million prize pool for esports tournaments.

- Enjoy LTMs? Well, 50v50 was the very first LTM in Battle Royale, released back in December 2017.

- Chapter 1 Season 1 was the only Season not to have a Battle Pass.

DRESS TO IMPRESS

Thanks to Fortnite's third-person perspective, the Outfit you choose to play in is always in view. So it makes sense that you want to be as sharp and stylish as possible on-screen! Chapter 2 has continued to produce hundreds of high-quality Outfits and associated variants from a huge variety of themes and looks. From eye-catching new anime looks to a soccer star, futuristic robots, and a dude with pancakes for a head, there's always an Outfit to intrigue you in the Item Shop or as part of the Battle Pass.

SET TO IT

As well as the Outfits themselves, a "Set" can feature a range of associated accessories such as Back Blings, Gliders, and Harvesting Tools. Rock a matching look, but equally don't be afraid to mix and match items from different Sets to show off your unique dress sense. Also, don't forget to explore any selectable Styles an Outfit may boast.

SPIRE ASSASSIN

Part of the Chapter 2 Season 6 Battle Pass, the eye-catching Spire Assassin is from the Looming Spire Set. Described as a "Guardian of a world beyond reality," this Legendary Outfit rocks a fearsome and futuristic look, ready for the Primal Season.

AGENT JONES

From the same Season, this Epic-rarity Outfit is a sharp look for the ever-adventurous Agent Jones. It had a further five unlockable Styles, seeing its sharp suit transition to more rough-and-ready attire.

CLUCK

If you needed more incentive to get involved with the Battle Pass, then this "eggsplosive" Chapter 2 Season 6 Battle Pass Outfit should do it! Cluck had two more Styles to unlock, including the Slurp-inspired Slurpy Style.

MAVE

A conspicuous Outfit from the Chapter 2 Season 5 Battle Pass, there's more to Mave than meets the... legs! You see, she has a reactive element that turns her legs into a big fin when she's swimming. Neat touch, huh? Mave also has the Unstoppable and Shieldbreaker Styles, which change up the look of her armor and ramp up her fear factor.

REESE

If you're looking for advanced tech, then this intergalactic Outfit ticks all the boxes. Another eye-catching inclusion in the Chapter 2: Season 5 Battle Pass, Reese shows off a cool range of body armor. When she's teamed with the Ne'Jari Warhammer Pickaxe and Dynamo Grav-Suit Back Bling, Reese totally locks down a look that says she means business in battle.

MANCAKE

Regular players will know that Fortnite has a long tradition of weird and wonderful cosmetics. Residing at Chapter 2 Season 5's Butter Barn, Mancake ticks both these boxes—he has a head made of pancakes and is dripping in syrup and butter! Throw in his Wild West-themed getup and Mancake is an Outfit that will live long in the memory.

LEXA

Obtained at level 73 of the Chapter 2 Season 5 Battle Pass, Lexa was the first in a new style of anime-inspired Battle Royale Outfits. The Fortnite community went wild for her simple yet striking style. She was later followed by Orin, another cartoon-like creation.

OLD SCHOOL

In Chapter 2 Season 4, the Origins Set introduced Outfits based on familiar faces from Chapter 1, including Jonesy The First, Wildstreak One, and Headhunter Prime.

KIT

An Outfit that's much lower on the fear factor scale is Kit, from Chapter 2 Season 3. As the son of Chapter 2 Season 2's Meowscles, the mighty mini sits atop a motorbike robot suit and struts and purrs just like dad. Its "Happy" and "Action" Styles are based on Meowscles' Ghost and Shadow Styles, respectively.

JULES

Has Jules's look been engineered for a show of stealth and power? Absolutely—she's a tough-as-titanium welder with no time for fakers and timewasters. Coming from the Intrepid Engines set, the Wrenchers Harvesting Tool perfectly caps off her stern facade.

AGENT PEELY

When Chapter 2 Season 2 debuted, Agent Peely appeared on our screens for the first time, and what a memorable moment that was! Who would have thought that slipping on a suit jacket, button shirt, and bowtie would elevate you to the rank of a secret agent? It did just the job for Peely.

METAL TEAM LEADER

Part of the Metal Team Leader Pack and classed as a member of the Royale Hearts Set, this lovable but lethal robot also came with the Warning Bow Back Bling for extra glitz. Not to be confused with the similar-sounding Mecha Team Leader, from the Final Showdown Set.

MIDAS REX

Midas Rex was included in the Last Laugh Bundle. If the original Midas, from the Chapter 2 Season 2 Battle Pass, wasn't enough of a steely-eyed assailant, Midas Rex added an extra dose of toughness with his full-length mecha suit. A simply awesome Outfit!

MENACE

Menace by name and menacing by nature. If you're going to parade around rocking a gladiator helmet and other golden garb, then you've got to be able to back up your gestures with genuine actions. Menace is well capable of that.

GALAXIA

As the exclusive Outfit in the first Fortnite Crew Pack, released during Chapter 2 Season 5, Galaxia has secured her spot as a highly-regarded cosmetic. Perhaps taking her cue from Outfits like Galaxy and Brite Bomber, Galaxia is packed with her own classy mix of color, glitz, and sparkle.

DUMMY

First seen in the Item Shop in Chapter 2 Season 3 and then making regular returns, Dummy is no fool when it comes to testing out the opposition. He has a simple and slim feel, although the selectable Carbon Fiber Style gives him a tougher hi-tech configuration. Pair him with the Wrong Turn Back Bling.

DOZER

Don't get caught snoozing on the job, dudes! Dozer needs to stay wide-eyed on the battlefield, just as the enemy will be when faced with Dozer's multicolored onesie sporting synthetic eyes and wings. The gear looks comfortable, obviously, but make sure it's not so cozy that you zonk out during a mission.

BOUNDLESS SET HEROES

Chapter 2 Season 4 was full of superheroes, including those from the Boundless Set. The Boundless Set Outfits came with hundreds of selectable options and combinations, covering areas like suit, mask, belt, pattern, and eyes. Heroes of the Boundless Set include Backlash, Blastoff, Dynamo Dancer, Firebrand, Hunter, Hypersonic, Joltara, The Mighty Volt, Polarity, and Wanderlust.

COBB

A rare Outfit that first popped up in the Item Shop in Chapter 2 Season 4, players moved quickly to get this in their Locker. There's nothing wrong with having a laugh on the Island, but thankfully Cobb also knows when it's time to get down to business. That said...a giant corncob with a smirky grin? You can't be serious.

ESSENTIAL EXTRAS

FLAPJACK FLYER

Mancake wouldn't be seen dropping in without his trusty Glider in tow! The Breakfast Bandit Set is full of tasty treats.

PHANTASMIC PULSE

From the superb Boundless Set, this Harvesting Tool is like no other and was a huge hit with fans.

EXPLODING AXIS

The Edge Factor Set in Chapter 2 Season 5 was futuristic and fancy, with this Back Bling really making a point!

BOOMBOX 3000

Carry the fight to the Island and carry some top tunes, too. A retro-style Back Bling that stays on trend.

THE CHANGING ISLAND

TRACK THE MAP THROUGH CHAPTER 2

Chapter 2 saw a new Island introduced, changing the landscape from what we knew from Season X and the nine campaigns before it. Throughout this Chapter, locations, landmarks, and Points of Interest arrived and evolved, offering up adventures and challenges to test all who ventured across the map. The action continued to escalate as the Island became flooded, hosted the crystalline desert, and saw the construction of The Spire.

SWEATY SANDS

FORTOGRAPHY

Beginning in Chapter 2 Season 5, the Fortnite Team has encouraged players to share themed gameplay shots they captured themselves—called "Fortography." The community has showed off some great scenes!

32

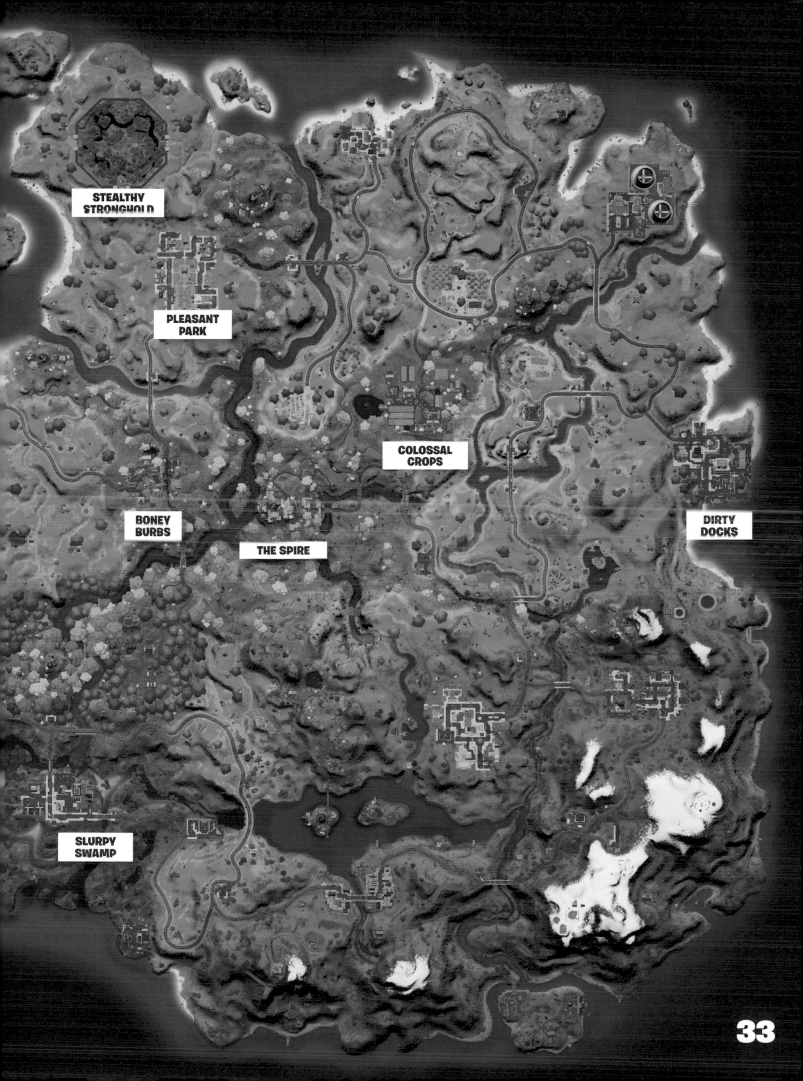

STEALTHY
STRONGHOLD

PLEASANT
PARK

COLOSSAL
CROPS

BONEY
BURBS

DIRTY
DOCKS

THE SPIRE

SLURPY
SWAMP

PLEASANT PARK

Returning to Chapter 2 Season 5, Pleasant Park has a mix of suburban space and small buildings to loot and spy from. It's one of the original locations from 2017, and as such always draws new and old fans alike in search of the rewards it can offer.

COLOSSAL CROPS

Showing remnants of Colossal Coliseum from Chapter 2 Season 5, Colossal Crops soon became a much-visited place the following Season. Sitting to the northeast of the central Spire, it shares the autumnal feel of the rest of the primal biome and is home to a mix of farmland and architecture.

THE SPIRE

The most recognizable location from Chapter 2 Season 6, The Spire and its surrounding village dominated the view. Surrounded by a scene of orangey-red natural features, it's a busy place for most of the game and offers rewards and riches to help you in battle. Bringing an Orb to this place offered you the Mythic-rarity Spire Jump Boots.

STEALTHY STRONGHOLD

Head to the northeast of the map to experience this interesting location. Beyond the huge walls lay stacks of trees, clearings, and a smattering of ruins. Catching unsuspecting opposition is possible when hidden among the jungle-like features. A mysterious pod showed up here during Chapter 2 Season 5.

SLURPY SWAMP

When the floodwaters of Chapter 2 Season 3 receded, this healing paradise was restored to its former glory. Head here for a revitalizing dip in the waters and enter the factory for a big boost to your Shield points. Treat the Slurp tanks as a regenerative miracle for you and your squad!

BONEY BURBS

Head out west from The Spire and you'll enter the slightly archaic arena that is Boney Burbs. Added in Chapter 2 Season 6 in place of Salty Towers, this location is a primarily urban zone with lots to explore. Duck between the range of buildings, taking care not to leave yourself open to a sniper attack.

DIRTY DOCKS

Way out east, Dirty Docks can be a quiet place due to its remote coastal location, but don't let that put you off a fun venture here. It remains a well-respected area ever since its Chapter 2 Season 1 arrival, and you can use the cranes and warehouses to gain good sighting spots.

SWEATY SANDS

Loaded with coveted loot Chests, Sweaty Sands should always be a location to consider when dropping from the Battle Bus. The pier attracts many visitors, and the hotel and neat houses are also worth checking out. Hop north to Coral Castle when you're done visiting here.

ICONIC LOCATIONS

THE CHAPTER 2 PLACES WE KNOW AND LOVED

ZERO POINT

The Zero Point dominated the middle of the map in Chapter 2 Season 5, with the encompassing desert area presenting a change in terrain. Visitors were wise to be aware of the sinking sand, where one could find cover in battle. A heightened sense of enemy detection was helpful here.

COLOSSAL COLISEUM

If you planned to head here, did you walk in through the entrance, or ramp over the imposing walls? Whatever way you approached this gladiatorial ground, you needed to be prepared for attacks from multiple angles. Also, because the layout of the coliseum's interior took different forms, you had to stay on your toes when entering.

THE AGENCY

Occupying the center of the map, the Agency was the home of Ghost and a heavily protected spot with Henchmen, turrets, and the boss Midas. This intimidating stone structure saw its demise during The Device event and became The Authority, which was guarded by Shadow.

THE RIG

Lurking beyond Slurpy Swamp, The Rig oil platform wasn't as scary as other places, but it still had an ominous atmosphere. The flood put this place fully out of commission, turning it into the run-down "Rickety Rig."

THE FORTILLA

After the flood struck, the Fortilla appeared as a Ghost base to help the organization adjust to the new way of Island life. Outsiders had to be careful, though, since Ghost Henchmen guarded this location.

BACK IN THE DAY

THE CHAPTER 1 POIs THAT ARE GONE BUT NOT FORGOTTEN

SNOBBY SHORES

Found out west (in fact, Snobby Shores was the most extreme westerly POI during its entire existence), this place was a luxurious mix of houses and buildings during Chapter 1. With its fancy houses as well as a pool, visitors enjoyed a sense of calm strolling through the neat streets. It was almost a shame when it got rampaged for mats and chests and became a backdrop for coastal conflict. The snobby residents didn't take kindly to that!

PARADISE PALMS

If you like Chapter 2's Sweaty Sands, then Paradise Palms may have been a spot you preferred to drop at back in Chapter 1. Being set in a vast desert, it was certainly a hot spot. It had a hotel, pool, and smart buildings all around. The top of the hotel building was a great place to land.

TOMATO TOWN

Tomato Town was a location that debuted in Chapter 1 Season 1. Located in the northeast, it became Tomato Temple in Season 5. Fans loved raiding the Uncle Pete's Pizza Pit restaurant and the gas station for goodies and steadily moving through the streets for rewards.

GREASY GROVE

Greasy Grove was a location that moved in and out of Fortnite during Chapter 1. During this time, this mix of traditional suburban streets saw floods and then a harsh frozen landscape, but players kept rocking on up to this westerly outpost in search of loot. The famous Durrr Burger restaurant was its most iconic landmark.

TILTED TOWERS

In Chapter 2 Season 5, Tilted Towers came back to form part of Salty Towers, but in its Chapter 1 pomp this was the place to hang out if you were after all-out action. The collection of high-rise towers and the high volume of people dropping here meant the race to grab a weapon was always frantic.

ENJOY THE RIDE

THE NEED FOR SPEED

The Shopping Cart was great fun for you and a buddy to mess around in, and the All Terrain Kart (ATK) allowed four players to move with more speed. But these Chapter 1 additions, which also included the Quadcrasher, weren't the kind of vehicles players would typically take on the road. That changed in Chapter 2 Season 3, when four awesome motors suddenly revved into action!

The Joy Ride update saw four new vehicles arrive and give you the chance to turn every day into a race day. Speeding across the Island's roads and fields means that evading the Storm and the enemy can be done much more quickly, though you need to keep an eye on the fuel, of course. You can also use them to join in the fun vehicle-based LTMs. So get behind the wheel and put the pedal to the metal!

MEET THE MOTORS

FORTNITE'S FINEST LAND-BASED CRUISERS

ISLANDER PREVALENT

This family sedan will carry a driver and three passengers at a decent speed and help your squad reach its goals. While it's nothing sporty, it still beats sprinting in the open and making yourself a target.

VICTORY MOTORS WHIPLASH

Compactness seems to create speed and style, but it also means only two players can cruise in the Whiplash. The Whiplash also has a handy boost function to massively increase its acceleration; however, deploying this will drain the fuel tank.

TITANO MUDFLAP

Acceleration and agility are not high on this truck's list of plus points; however, it still does a "smashing" job on the map. The Titano Mudflap can flatten player builds and cause significant ram damage. Like the OG Bear pickup, it has high Health so if you're fuelled up, this beast can be a total game changer.

OG BEAR

The game's not all about pretty roads and pounding the tarmac—sometimes you've got to go off the beaten track and drive a little wild. The OG Bear pickup copes better than other cars when on the rough stuff and has a greater fuel capacity. It carries four people, which is also a bonus.

ON THE MOVE

During Chapter 2, the theme of "being on the move" was prevalent in other ways, too. The Spy Games LTM Operation: Payload challenged teams of eight to either escort a valuable truck to its destination or stop it at all costs! Achieving your mission secured you Intel and unlocked Tech. Tech was a bunch of special gear and skills you could use in other Spy Games LTMs, including a jetpack and double jump ability.

TAKE THE TRANSPORT

MORE OF THE MACHINES THAT MAKE YOU MOVE

CHOPPA

In Chapter 2 Season 2, the Choppa flew into action to make the skies a battleground. A squad could open fire on enemies below but had to be aware that this big machine was itself a target from land-based strikes. Moving quickly and keeping close to hillsides was the best way to utilize the Choppa.

MOTORBOAT

The waters influenced so much of Chapter 2, so fortunately the powerful Motorboat cruised by to help players navigate them. With four seats and a speed boost option, it can even be deployed across the land if the driver knows how to handle it and limit the damage. One of the Motorboat's biggest appeals is the onboard missiles.

B.R.U.T.E.

Grab a buddy and jump in this giant mech suit as one of you steers and the other powers the guns. It's up there as perhaps one of the craziest vehicles ever—B.R.U.T.E. was an absolute game changer in Season X for its short-lived reign.

THE BALLER

Unique in many ways, The Baller was a vehicle that offered protection to the solo occupant and moved towards its target after the grappler attached itself to it. Coming to Battle Royale in Season 8, it existed alongside the Driftboard, which was another single-player vehicle.

X-4 STORMWING

In Chapter 2 Season 5's Operation Snowdown winter event, players once again had a chance to experience the flying thrills of the classy X-4 Stormwing plane. This agile fan favorite, often called the "biplane," first appeared in Chapter 1 Season 7.

BACK TO THE DRAWING BOARD
HOW TO DRAW: LEXA

1 Start by drawing this Epic Outfit by lightly sketching Lexa's basic framework.

2 Add shape to your figure, keeping her posture in mind. Her body is angled confidently, with a strong standing stance.

3 Using your guides, begin to sketch the outline of the body. Introduce shape in the arms and legs and some finer facial details.

4 Time to suit up and sketch the armor. Each section can be broken into basic angular shapes to make the task less daunting.

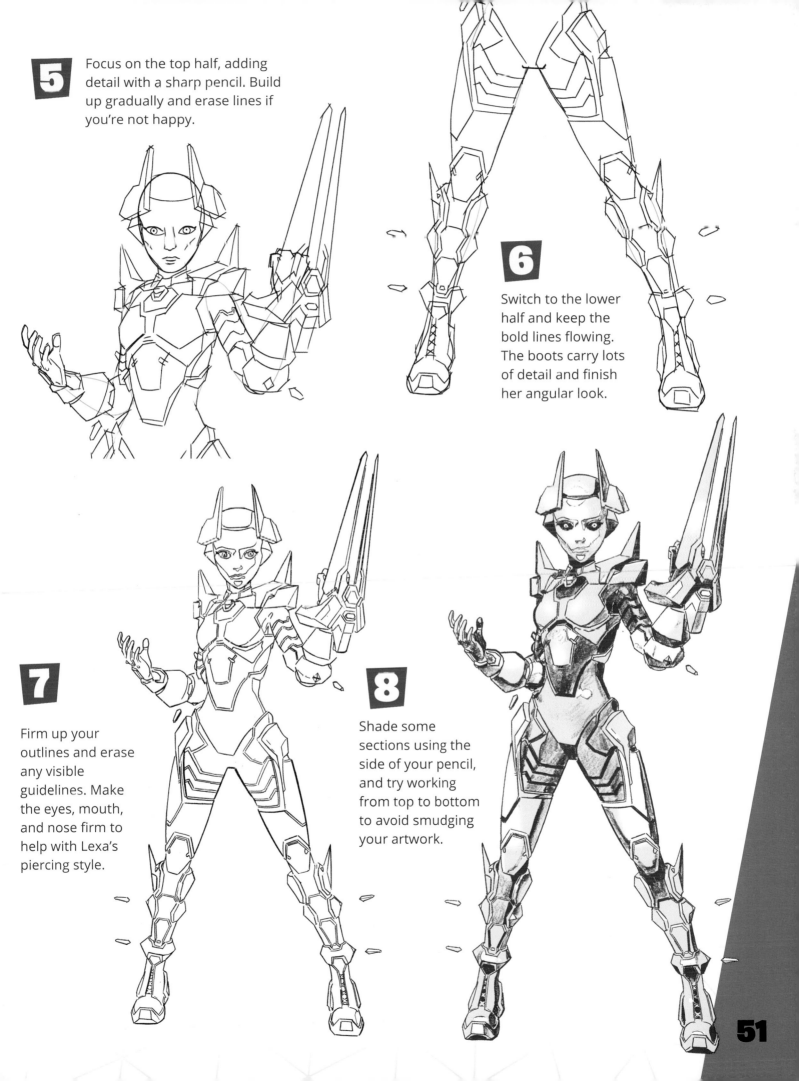

5 Focus on the top half, adding detail with a sharp pencil. Build up gradually and erase lines if you're not happy.

6 Switch to the lower half and keep the bold lines flowing. The boots carry lots of detail and finish her angular look.

7 Firm up your outlines and erase any visible guidelines. Make the eyes, mouth, and nose firm to help with Lexa's piercing style.

8 Shade some sections using the side of your pencil, and try working from top to bottom to avoid smudging your artwork.

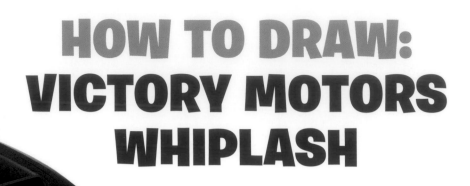

HOW TO DRAW: VICTORY MOTORS WHIPLASH

1 Start with a very simple and clean basic outline of the two-seater sports car.

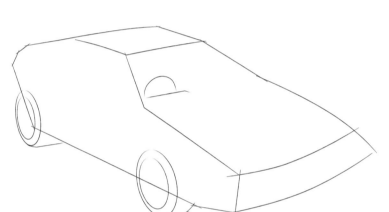

2 Add two wheels, with accurate circles for the rims and tires. The tires are medium width. Erase your circles if you're not happy and keep trying until you are.

3 Time for details, including wheel arches, mirrors, rear spoiler, and the large scoop on the hood.

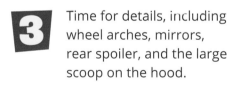

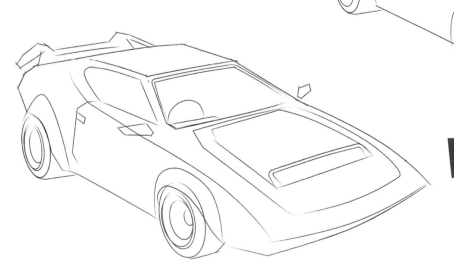

4 Sketch in more bodywork details like the door panel and the raised position of the front scoop. Add depth to the wheels.

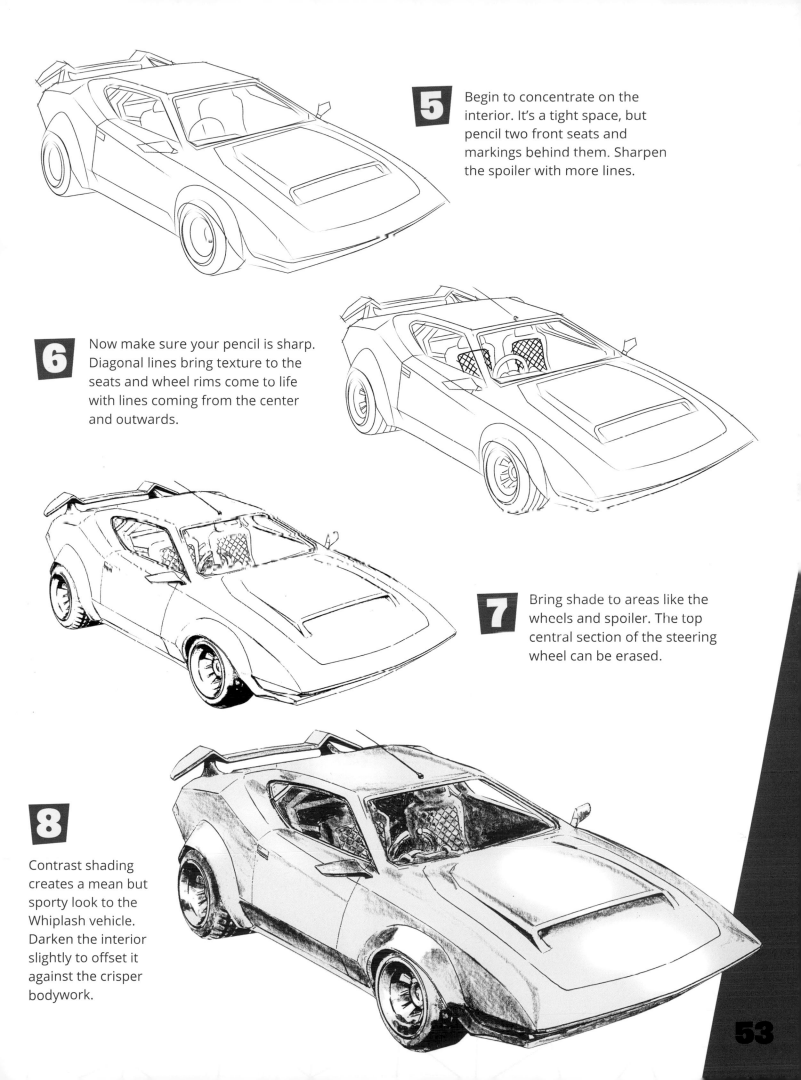

5 Begin to concentrate on the interior. It's a tight space, but pencil two front seats and markings behind them. Sharpen the spoiler with more lines.

6 Now make sure your pencil is sharp. Diagonal lines bring texture to the seats and wheel rims come to life with lines coming from the center and outwards.

7 Bring shade to areas like the wheels and spoiler. The top central section of the steering wheel can be erased.

8 Contrast shading creates a mean but sporty look to the Whiplash vehicle. Darken the interior slightly to offset it against the crisper bodywork.

53

COMBAT CHOICES

CRAFTY MOVES

Knowing how to craft your own advanced items could really give you the upper hand during the primal times of Chapter 2 Season 6. The option to craft weapons could take you and your squad's firepower to a new level as you mixed up a winning move.

The arrival of Exotic weapons, occurring in Chapter 2 Season 5, was also big news. Getting your hands on one of these could add an extra dimension to your combat technique—the Dragon's Breath Shotgun and Night Hawk Revolver, for example, had special powers to draw upon in battle. Chapter 2 was also loaded with other exciting weapons and items, such as the Charge Shotgun and Lever Action Rifle.

PRIMAL RIFLE

Known for its high damage, two elements are needed to craft this very handy weapon, namely a Makeshift Rifle and Animal Bones. Crafting it is easily done by opening the Crafting tab in the menu and making the right selection.

PRIMAL SHOTGUN

This returned at the beginning of Chapter 2 Season 6, both as loot and as part of the Crafting feature. Makeshift weapons have the ability to be crafted into familiar favorites such as the Pump Shotgun, Revolver, and Assault Rifle. This method of crafting requires Mechanical Parts harvested from machinery.

DRAGON'S BREATH SHOTGUN

Added in Epic and Legendary rarities in Chapter 2 Season 5, things get a little hot under the collar when this shotgun is in use. Targets go up in flames when hit, meaning that enemies can be flushed out from burning builds in a close-quarters game. The Dragon's Breath Sniper Rifle—an Exotic—works in the same way, with a single long-range strike turning up the heat on the opposition.

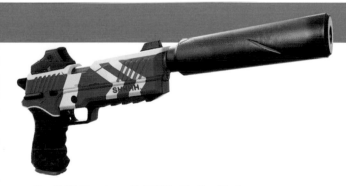

BOOM SNIPER RIFLE

In Chapter 2 Season 5, meeting up with the Character Splode gave you the chance to trade Bars for this beauty! Firing clingers, the Boom Sniper's ammo attaches to your enemy and then explodes within a couple of seconds for maximum impact. A long-range weapon you can easily become attached to.

SHADOW TRACKER

Sporting a sweet red and white design, this Exotic pistol was another welcome addition to Chapter 2 Season 5. Traded from Reese and then Power Chord, the Shadow Tracker's top trick is marking the whereabouts of your target so the rest of your squad can join the action. There's no hiding in the shadows now!

NIGHT HAWK REVOLVER

Catching up with Mancake at Butter Barn meant you could trade for this awesome revolver with a neat thermal scope. The Night Hawk is great in mid-range combat, and the thermal finder aids you in homing in on a tricky target. It's especially effective in the Storm when identifying the enemy under difficult circumstances.

STORM SCOUT SNIPER RIFLE

Chapter 1 players will recall the original Storm Scout weapon, which used a built-in weather map to warn of the upcoming Storm movements. Well, the Chapter 2 Season 5 Storm Scout Sniper Rifle brought back this handy trick. A trip to trade with Lexa saw you collect this useful weapon.

KIT'S SHOCKWAVE LAUNCHER

Defeating Kit in Chapter 2 Season 3 wasn't easy, but the reward was picking up Kit's Shockwave Launcher and causing havoc with its powers. Launching explosive Shockwave Grenades at the enemy would fling them in all directions, and it could also be used on your own squad to quickly move them away from danger. Fun and frantic.

JULES' GLIDER GUN

Despite the name, this isn't actually a weapon... but it was an Item that still gave you the upper hand in Chapter 2 Season 3! Working similarly to the original Grappler, it could be fired and used to pull a player towards their target. Glider redeploy was available using this, so eliminating Jules to grab this item was a great boost.

BURST QUAD LAUNCHER

Delving back into the Exotic weapons, the Burst Quad Launcher was a fun explosive weapon collected from Fishstick in Chapter 2 Season 5. Sporting a menacing look, it blasted four rockets per shot and was a beast to have by your side.

LEVER ACTION SHOTGUN

Coming in every type from Common to Legendary, this weapon carries a high damage rate, but you do have to allow for the reload time.

PROXIMITY MINE

You had to make sure you "stuck" to your task with the proximity mine! Released in Chapter 2 Season 2, this explosive needed to be attached to a surface and then, once hit with a weapon or walked over, it would explode and cause damage. Surfaces it could stick to included vehicles.

BATTLE ROYALE RECORD

KEEP TRACK OF YOUR GAME GLORY

CHAPTER & SEASON:

....

PLATFORM PLAYING ON:

....

LOCATIONS WE DROPPED:

....

....

....

SQUAD MEMBERS:

....

....

....

....

....

DATE:

....

LOCKER:

OUTFIT

....

GLIDER

....

BACK BLING

....

HARVESTING TOOL

....

EMOTES

....

TACTICS:

....

....

....

....

....

....

....

LOADOUT:

....

....

....

....

....

KEY STATS:

MOST ELIMINATIONS IN A GAME

....

MOST ELIMINATIONS IN A DAY

....

FINAL PLACEMENTS

....

VICTORY ROYALES EARNED:

....

FORTNITE FAVES

FAVORITE LTMS:

....
....
....
....
....
....

FAVORITE WEAPONS:

....
....
....
....
....
....

FAVORITE TACTICS:

....

....

....

....

FAVORITE VEHICLE:

....

....

....

....

FAVORITE CREATORS & STREAMERS:

....

....

....

....

FAVORITE OUTFIT:

....

....

....

....

FAVORITE LOCATIONS:

....

....

....

....

FAVORITE CREATIVE HUBS:

....

....

....

....

BOOGIE IN BATTLE

MAKE YOUR MOVE WITH THESE CHAPTER 2 EMOTES

Whether you pick them up in the Item Shop, unlock them through the Battle Pass, or use a built-in one with an Outfit, Emotes continue to be a big part of Battle Royale through Chapter 2. Getting your groove on is an entertaining factor of the game—many fans plan their celebrations in advance and carefully coordinate a routine with their squad. In Chapter 2 Season 5, exclusive built-in Emotes included Mancake's slippery Syrup Slinger move and Lexa's Hunter Protocol display.

DECIDE YOUR DANCE

BOOMIN'

Unlocked at Level 16 of the Chapter 2 Season 5 Battle Pass, Boomin' plays tunes from a large boombox. Walk around and dance as you carry it.

OFFICE CHARIOT

You don't even need to stand up to bust out this move—just swing and sway on your office chair and the job is done!

IT'S COMPLICATED

Like things a bit complex? It's Complicated has quick flicks and tricks, so move at speed to get people watching.

JUMBO POPCORN

Arriving in tandem with Party Royale's Short Nite event, this Emote's for all the big screen fans out there munching through their favorite refreshment while watching movies!

MORE MEGA MOVERS

A WARRIOR PREPARES

How should a warrior prepare in Battle Royale? By getting down on one knee, picking up some dirt, and rubbing it in their hands.

SHANTY FOR A SQUAD

Released in Chapter 2 Season 5, this catchy Emote is a big hit in Squads mode. As more players perform the Emote in close proximity, the more layers are added to the music.

SYRUP SLINGER

A built-in Emote for Mancake, he's soon drenched in syrup after flashing his bottle around. A pretty "sweet" maneuver.

SWOLE CAT

From the Swole Cat Set, this built-in Emote sees Meowscles power pose. One, two, three, and...flex!

HIGH FIVE

Battle Royale's first "Synced" Emote, this is a high five you can pull off with another player. Time to raise those digits!

MEMBERS ONLY

Debuting in Fortnite Crew, this is another Synced Emote—just go up to someone and begin the elaborate hand clapping, even if they aren't a member of Fortnite Crew.

STORMY

Maybe the Emote that requires the least activity—just stand under a cloud, look ultra moody, and soak up the storm!

MASHED POTATO

Go low, go high, and flap your feet and hands. This Chapter 2 Season 5 Emote is as easy as mashing a potato.

FORTNITE QUIZ

TEST YOUR BATTLE ROYALE BRAIN

TACKLE ALL 25 QUESTIONS TO SEE HOW YOU SCORE

COMMON

BASIC BATTLE ROYALE TESTS   (ONE point per correct answer)

1.   What is the name of the big blue machine players drop from at the beginning of a match? ....

2.   What is the storage box containing loot such as weapons and Health items called? ....

3.   Give the nickname for Chapter 2 Season 2. ....

4.   Which of the following is NOT a building material in Fortnite: Bamboo, Wood, Metal, or Stone? ....

5.   Which two famous words describe an overall win in Fortnite? ....

UNCOMMON
TIME TO GET TOUGHER (TWO points per correct answer)

6. What's the Fortnite in-game currency called?

....

7. Which of these is NOT a type of rarity: Legendary, Mythic, Exotic, or Fantasy?

....

8. Bear Force One, Cuddle Cruiser, and Fishy Flier are types of which cosmetic item?

....

9. The Tomatohead and PJ Pepperoni Outfits come from what Set?

....

10. What's the name of this reviving machine, which was first introduced in Chapter 1 Season 8?

....

RARE
STEP IT UP (THREE points per correct answer)

11. Name the throwable Item, first seen in Chapter 1 Season 5, that instantly unleashed a huge combat fort.

....

12. In what Season did TNTina make her debut?

....

13. What type of bullets does a Tactical Assault Rifle use?

....

14. Who is this?

....

15. In Creative, how many digits make up an Island Code?

....

FORTNITE QUIZ

EPIC

THINK HARD! (FOUR points per correct answer)

16. On the original Chapter 1 map, which was furthest south: Flush Factory, Salty Springs, or Greasy Grove?

....

17. What Season Battle Pass had the tagline "X Marks the Spot"?

....

18. Who won the Solo 2019 Fortnite World Cup?

....

19. Pirate and Gold were unlockable Styles for what Pet? (A Pet is a type of Back Bling.)

....

20. The Visitor, The Scientist, and The Paradigm are in what Set?

....

LEGENDARY

DEEP BREATHS... THIS IS TOTALLY TRICKY! (FIVE points per correct answer)

21. Name the northern Chapter 1 location full of old cars and scrap metal.

....

22. What is the magazine size of the Lever Action Rifle?

....

23. In what Season was the Shopping Cart vehicle vaulted?

....

24. What were the mysterious purple items that reduced visibility, increased speed, and let a player pass through solid objects?

....

25. Can you name the official in-game trophy for the FNCS Champions in competitive play, first announced in Chapter 2 Season 2?

....

ANSWERS: 1. Battle Bus, 2. Chest, 3. Top Secret, 4. Bamboo, 5. V-Bucks, 6. Victory Royale, 7. Fantasy, 8. Glider, 9. Pizza Pit, 10. Reboot Van, 11. Point a Fortrace, 12. Chapter 2 Season 2, 13. Light bullets, 14. Snowmando, 15. 12, 16. Flush Factory, 17. Chapter 1 Season 8, 18. Kyle 'Bugha' Giersdorf, 19. Woodsy, 20. The Seven, 21. Junk Junction, 22. 9, 23. Chapter 1 Season 9, 24. Shadow stones, 25. Axe of Champions.

WHAT WAS YOUR SCORE?

Add up your total quiz points and look below to see how you rank in Battle Royale...

0-15	16-30	31-45	46-60	61-74	75
You still have a lot to learn, but don't give up!	You know the basics but there's room for improvement. Keep trying!	You have a solid understanding of Fortnite. Be proud of your hard work!	A very impressive effort. You certainly know your way round the Island.	Such an amazing score—you only just missed the top level.	Every quiz question correct—nobody else rules the Island like you do!

First published in the UK in 2021 by WILDFIRE an imprint of
HEADLINE PUBLISHING GROUP

Cataloguing in Publication Data is available
from the British Library
Hardback 978 14722 8361 0

Written by Kevin Pettman
Design by Amazing15
How to draw illustrations by Mike Collins
All images © Epic Games, Inc.
Printed and bound in Italy by L.E.G.O. S.p.A.

HEADLINE PUBLISHING GROUP
An Hachette UK Company
Carmelite House
50 Victoria Embankment
London, EC4 0DZ
www.headline.co.uk www.hachette.co.uk

www.epicgames.com

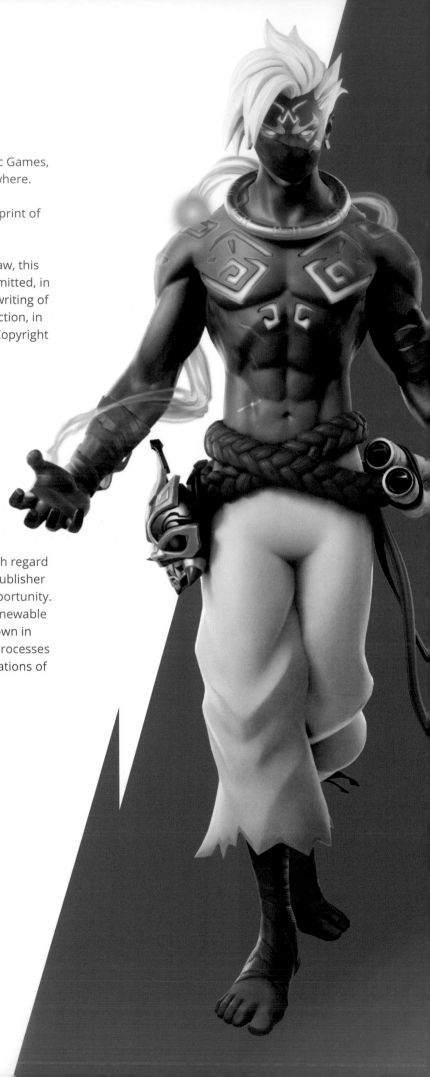